A·CHILD'S·
·GARDEN·
·OF·VERSES·

A CHILD'S GARDEN of VERSES

BY·ROB
-ERT·LOVIS
STEVENSON

ILLVS
-TRATED~
BY CHARLES
ROBINSON.

MAINSTREAM:
EDINBVRGH
WATERSTONE'S:
EDINBVRGH,
DVBLIN AND
LONDON

Copyright © this facsimile edition Mainstream 1990

Reprinted 1991, 1992, 1995, 1997, 1998, 2001, 2002, 2003, 2005

This edition, reproduced from the 1896 edition,
published in Great Britain in 1990 by
MAINSTREAM PUBLISHING COMPANY (EDINBURGH) LTD
7 Albany Street
Edinburgh EH1 3UG

ISBN 1 85158 391 2

A catalogue record for this book is
available from the British Library

Title-page lettering by Yvonne Holton

Printed and bound in Great Britain by
The Bath Press, Bath

T.º ALISON CUNNINGHAM.

FROM HER BOY . ᛒ . ᛒ . ᛒ .

FOR THE LONG NIGHTS YOU LAY AWAKE
    AND WATCHED FOR MY UNWORTHY SAKE:
    FOR YOUR MOST COMFORTABLE HAND
THAT LED ME THROUGH THE UNEVEN LAND:
FOR ALL THE STORY BOOKS YOU READ:
FOR ALL THE PAINS YOU COMFORTED:
FOR ALL YOU PITIED, ALL YOU BORE,
IN SAD AND HAPPY DAYS OF YORE:—
MY SECOND MOTHER, MY FIRST WIFE,
THE ANGEL OF MY INFANT LIFE—
FROM THE SICK CHILD, NOW WELL AND OLD,
TAKE, NURSE, THE LITTLE BOOK YOU HOLD!

AND GRANT IT, HEAVEN, THAT ALL WHO READ
MAY FIND AS DEAR A NURSE AT NEED,
AND EVERY CHILD WHO LISTS MY RHYME,
IN THE BRIGHT, FIRESIDE, NURSERY CLIME,
MAY HEAR IT IN AS KIND A VOICE
AS MADE MY CHILDISH DAYS REJOICE!

R. L. S.

CONTENTS

CONTENTS

CONTENTS

THE CHILD ALONE

CONTENTS

GARDEN DAYS

ENVOYS

A CHILD'S GARDEN of Verses . . . . .

BED
IN SUMMER

I N winter I get up at night
  And dress by yellow candle-light.
In summer, quite the other way,
I have to go to bed by day.

I have to go to bed and see
The birds still hopping on the tree,
Or hear the grown-up people's feet
Still going past me in the street.

3

BED IN SUMMER

And does it not seem hard to you,
When all the sky is clear and blue,
And I should like so much to play,
To have to go to bed by day?

IT is very nice to think
The world is full of
    meat and drink,
With little children
    saying grace
In every Christian
    kind of place.

A Thought.

WHEN I was down beside the sea
A wooden spade they gave to me
To dig the sandy shore .
My holes were empty like a cup ,
In every hole the sea came up ,
Till it could come no more .

At
The Seaside .

6

 YOUNG NIGHT THOUGHT.

ALL night long and every night,
When my mamma puts out the light,
I see the people marching by,
As plain as day, before my eye.

Armies and emperors and kings,
All carrying different kinds of things,
And marching in so grand a way,
You never saw the like by day.

So fine a show was never seen,
At the great circus on the green ;
For every kind of beast and man
Is marching in that caravan.

YOUNG NIGHT THOUGHT

At first they move a little slow,
But still the faster on they go,
And still beside them close I keep
Until we reach the town of Sleep.

WHOLE DUTY OF CHILDREN

A CHILD should always
        say what's true
And speak when
        he is spoken to,
And behave
        mannerly at table:
At least as far as he
        is able.

9

RAIN

THE rain is raining all around,
  It falls on field and tree,
It rains on the umbrellas here,
  And on the ships at sea.

·PIRATE STORY·

THREE of us afloat in the meadow by the
    swing,
  Three of us aboard in the basket on the lea.
Winds are in the air, they are blowing in the
      spring,
    And waves are on the meadow like the waves
      there are at sea.

Where shall we adventure to-day that we're afloat,
    Wary of the weather and steering by a star?
Shall it be to Africa, a-steering of the boat,
    To Providence, or Babylon, or off to Malabar?

11

Hi ! but here's a squadron a-rowing on the sea—
  Cattle on the meadow a-charging with a roar !
Quick, and we'll escape them, they're as mad as
    they can be,
    The wicket is the harbour and the garden is
      the shore.

FOREIGN LANDS

UP into the cherry tree
Who should climb but little me?
I held the trunk with both my hands
And looked abroad on foreign lands.

I saw the next door garden lie,
Adorned with flowers before my eye,
And many pleasant places more
That I had never seen before.

13

FOREIGN LANDS

I saw the dimpling river pass
And be the sky's blue looking-glass;
The dusty roads go up and down
With people tramping in to town.

If I could find a higher tree
Farther and farther I should see,
To where the grown-up river slips
Into the sea among the ships,

To where the roads on either hand
Lead onward into fairy land,
Where all the children dine at five,
And all the playthings come alive.

WINDY·NIGHTS

HENEVER the moon and stars
    are set,
Whenever the wind is high,
All night long in the dark and wet,
  A man goes riding by.
Late in the night when the fires are out,
Why does he gallop and gallop about?

WINDY NIGHTS

Whenever the trees are crying aloud,
  And ships are tossed at sea,
By, on the highway, low and loud,
  By at the gallop goes he;
By at the gallop he goes, and then
By he comes back at the gallop again.

TRAVELS

I SHOULD like to rise and go
    Where the golden apples grow;—
Where below another sky
Parrot islands anchored lie,
And, watched by cockatoos and goats,
Lonely Crusoes building boats;—
Where in sunshine reaching out
Eastern cities, miles about,
Are with mosque and minaret
Among sandy gardens set,
And the rich goods from near and far
Hang for sale in the bazaar;—

17

TRAVEL

Where the Great Wall round China goes,
And on one side the desert blows,
And with bell and voice and drum,
Cities on the other hum ;—
Where are forests, hot as fire,
Wide as England, tall as a spire,
Full of apes and cocoa-nuts
And the negro hunters' huts ;—
Where the knotty crocodile
Lies and blinks in the Nile,
And the red flamingo flies
Hunting fish before his eyes ;—
Where in jungles near and far,
Man-devouring tigers are,
Lying close and giving ear
Lest the hunt be drawing near,
Or a comer-by be seen
Swinging in a palanquin :—
Where among the desert sands
Some deserted city stands,
All its children, sweep and prince,
Grown to manhood ages since,
Not a foot in street or house,
Not a stir of child or mouse,
And when kindly falls the night,
In all the town no spark of light.
There I'll come when I'm a man
With a camel caravan ;
Light a fire in the gloom
Of some dusty dining-room ;

TRAVEL

See the pictures on the walls,
Heroes, fights and festivals;
And in a corner find the toys
Of the old Egyptian boys.

SINGING

OF speckled eggs the birdie sings
  And nests among the trees;
The sailor sings of ropes and things
  In ships upon the seas.

The children sing in far Japan,
  The children sing in Spain;
The organ with the organ man
  Is singing in the rain.

"OF SPECKLED EGGS THE BIRDIE SINGS."

LOOK-
-ING

FOR-
-WARD

WHEN I am grown to man's estate
    I shall be very proud and great,
And tell the other girls and boys
Not to meddle with my toys.

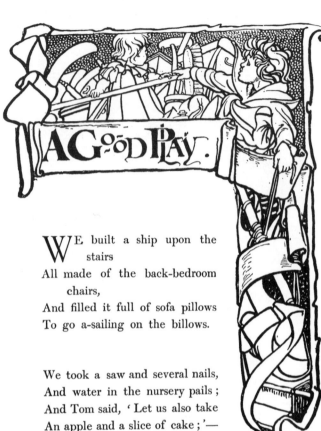

A GOOD PLAY.

WE built a ship upon the
 stairs
All made of the back-bedroom
 chairs,
And filled it full of sofa pillows
To go a-sailing on the billows.

We took a saw and several nails,
And water in the nursery pails;
And Tom said, ' Let us also take
An apple and a slice of cake;'—
Which was enough for Tom and
 me
To go a-sailing on, till tea.

A GOOD PLAY

We sailed along for days and days,
And had the very best of plays;
But Tom fell out and hurt his knee,
So there was no one left but me.

WHERE GO THE - BOATS?

DARK brown is the river,
    Golden is the sand.
It flows along for ever,
    With trees on either hand.

Green leaves a-floating,
    Castles of the foam,
Boats of mine a-boating—
    Where will all come home?

On goes the river
    And out past the mill,
Away down the valley,
    Away down the hill.

WHERE GO THE BOATS?

Away down the river,
  A hundred miles or more,
Other little children
  Shall bring my boats ashore.

AUNTIE'S SKIRTS

Whenever
  Auntie moves
          around,
Her dresses
     make a
curious sound,

They trail
behind her up the
          floor,
And trundle
   after through
          the door.

The Land of Counterpane

WHEN I was sick and lay a-bed,
    I had two pillows at my head,
    And all my toys beside me lay
To keep me happy all the day.

And sometimes for an hour or so
I watched my leaden soldiers go,
With different uniforms and drills,
Among the bed-clothes, through the hills;

And sometimes sent my ships in fleets
All up and down among the sheets;
Or brought my trees and houses out,
And planted cities all about.

THE LAND OF COUNTERPANE

I was the giant great and still
That sits upon the pillow-hill,
And sees before him, dale and plain,
The pleasant land of counterpane.

·THE LAND ·
·OF· NOD ·

FROM breakfast on through all
the day
At home among my friends
I stay;
But every night I go abroad
Afar into the Land of Nod.

All by myself I have to go,
With none to tell me what to do—
All alone beside the streams
And up the mountain-sides of dreams.

"Up the
mountain
sides of
dreams."

30

THE LAND OF NOD

The strangest things are there for me,
Both things to eat and things to see,
And many frightening sights abroad
Till morning in the Land of Nod.

Try as I like to find the way,
I never can get back by day,
Nor can remember plain and clear
The curious music that I hear.

MY SHADOW

I HAVE a little shadow that goes in and out
    with me,
And what can be the use of him is more than I
    can see.
He is very, very like me from the heels up to
    the head ;
And I see him jump before me, when I jump
    into my bed.

The funniest thing about him is the way he likes
    to grow—
Not at all like proper children, which is always
    very slow ;
For he sometimes shoots up taller, like an india-
    rubber ball,
And he sometimes gets so little that there's none
    of him at all.

He hasn't got a notion of how children ought to
    play,
And can only make a fool of me in every sort of
    way.

MY SHADOW

He stays so close beside me, he's a coward you
    can see ;
I'd think shame to stick to nursie as that shadow
    sticks to me !

One morning, very early, before the sun was up,
I rose and found the shining dew on every but-
    tercup ;
But my lazy little shadow, like an arrant sleepy-
    head,
Had stayed at home behind me and was fast
    asleep in bed.

SYSTEM

EVERY night my prayers I say,
  And get my dinner every day;
  And every day that I've been good,
  I get an orange after food.

SYSTEM

The child that is not clean and neat,
With lots of toys and things to eat,
He is a naughty child, I'm sure—
Or else his dear papa is poor.

I WOKE before the morning, I was
happy all the day,
I never said an ugly word, but smiled and stuck
to play.

And now at last the sun is going down behind
the wood,
And I am very happy, for I know that I've been
good.

My bed is waiting cool and fresh, with linen
smooth and fair,
And I must off to sleepsin-by, and not forget my
prayer.

I know that, till to-morrow I shall see the sun
arise,
No ugly dream shall fright my mind, no ugly
sight my eyes,

36

A GOOD BOY

But slumber hold me tightly till I waken in the
    dawn,
And hear the thrushes singing in the lilacs round
    the lawn.

ESCAPE · AT · BEDTIME

THE lights from the parlour and
kitchen shone out
   Through the blinds and the windows
   and bars;
And high overhead and all moving
   about,
There were thousands of millions of stars.
There ne'er were such thousands of leaves on a
   tree,
   Nor of people in church or the Park,
As the crowds of the stars that looked down upon
   me,
   And that glittered and winked in the dark.

ESCAPE AT BEDTIME

The Dog, and the Plough, and the Hunter, and
    all,
  And the star of the sailor, and Mars,
These shone in the sky, and the pail by the wall,
  Would be half full of water and stars.
They saw me at last, and they chased me with
    cries,
  And they soon had me packed into bed ;
But the glory kept shining and bright in my eyes,
  And the stars going round in my head.

· MARCHING ~
~ SONG ·

BRING the comb and play upon it !
   Marching, here we come !
Willie cocks his highland bonnet,
   Johnnie beats the drum.

Mary Jane commands the party,
   Peter leads the rear ;
Fleet in time, alert and hearty,
   Each a Grenadier !

All in the most martial manner
   Marching double-quick ;
While the napkin like a banner
   Waves upon the stick !

MARCHING SONG

Here's enough of fame and pillage,
  Great commander Jane !
Now that we've been round the village,
  Let's go home again.

THE · COW ·

THE friendly cow all red and white,
   I love with all my heart:
She gives me cream with all her might,
   To eat with apple-tart.

THE COW

She wanders lowing here and there,
   And yet she cannot stray,
All in the pleasant open air,
   The pleasant light of day;

And blown by all the winds that pass
   And wet with all the showers,
She walks among the meadow grass
   And eats the meadow flowers.

HAPPY-
THOUGHT.

The world is so full
of a number of things,
I'm sure we should all
be as happy as kings.

THE WIND

I SAW you toss the kites on high
  And blow the birds about the sky;
And all around I heard you pass,
Like ladies' skirts across the grass—
    O wind, a-blowing all day long,
    O wind, that sings so loud a song!

I saw the different things you did,
But always you yourself you hid.
I felt you push, I heard you call,
I could not see yourself at all—
    O wind, a-blowing all day long,
    O wind, that sings so loud a song!

THE WIND

O you that are so strong and cold,
O blower, are you young or old?
Are you a beast of field and tree,
Or just a stronger child than me?
    O wind, a-blowing all day long,
    O wind, that sings so loud a song!

KEEPSAKE·MILL

OVER the borders, a sin without pardon,
　　Breaking the branches and crawling
　　　below,
Out through the breach in the wall of the garden,
　　Down by the banks of the river, we go.

Here is the mill with the humming of thunder,
　　Here is the weir with the wonder of foam,
Here is the sluice with the race running under—
　　Marvellous places, though handy to home !

Sounds of the village grow stiller and stiller,
　　Stiller the note of the birds on the hill ;
Dusty and dim are the eyes of the miller,
　　Deaf are his ears with the moil of the mill.

Years may go by, and the wheel in the river
　　Wheel as it wheels for us, children, to-day,
Wheel and keep roaring and foaming for ever
　　Long after all of the boys are away.

KEEPSAKE MILL

Home from the Indies and home from the ocean,
  Heroes and soldiers we all shall come home;
Still we shall find the old mill wheel in motion,
  Turning and churning that river to foam.

You with the bean that I gave when we
    quarrelled,
  I with your marble of Saturday last,
Honoured and old and all gaily apparelled,
  Here we shall meet and remember the past.

"THE · BEAN · THAT · I · GAVE · WHEN · WE ·
QUARRELLED".

CHILDREN, you are very little,
And your bones are very brittle;
If you would grow great and stately,
You must try to walk sedately.

You must still be bright and quiet,
And content with simple diet;
And remain, through all bewild'ring,
Innocent and honest children.

Happy hearts and happy faces,
Happy play in grassy places—
That was how, in ancient ages,
Children grew to kings and sages.

But the unkind and the unruly,
And the sort who eat unduly,
They must never hope for glory—
Theirs is quite a different story!

GOOD AND BAD CHILDREN

Cruel children, crying babies,
All grow up as geese and gabies,
Hated, as their age increases,
By their nephews and their nieces.

FOREIGN CHILDREN

L ITTLE Indian, Sioux or Crow,
Little frosty Eskimo,
Little Turk or Japanee,
O! don't you wish that you were me?

You have seen the scarlet trees
And the lions over seas;
You have eaten ostrich eggs,
And turned the turtles off their legs.

Such a life is very fine,
But it's not so nice as mine:
You must often, as you trod,
Have wearied *not* to be abroad.

51

FOREIGN CHILDREN

You have curious things to eat,
I am fed on proper meat;
You must dwell beyond the foam,
But I am safe and live at home.

Little Indian, Sioux or Crow,
Little frosty Eskimo,
Little Turk or Japanee,
O! don't you wish that you were me?

·THE SUN'S· ·TRAVELS·

HE sun is not a-bed, when I
At night upon my pillow lie;
Still round the earth his way
he takes,
And morning after morning makes.

While here at home, in shining day,
We round the sunny garden play,
Each little Indian sleepy-head
Is being kissed and put to bed.

And when at eve I rise from tea,
Day dawns beyond the Atlantic Sea,
And all the children in the West
Are getting up and being dressed.

THE
LAMP-
LIGHTER·

MY tea is nearly ready and the sun has left
the sky;
It's time to take the window to see Leerie going
by;
For every night at tea-time and before you take
your seat,
With lantern and with ladder he comes posting up
the street.

Now Tom would be a driver and Maria go to sea,
And my papa's a banker and as rich as he
can be;
But I, when I am stronger and can choose what
I'm to do,
O Leerie, I'll go round at night and light the
lamps with you!

For we are very lucky, with a lamp before the
door,
And Leerie stops to light it as he lights so many
more ;
And O! before you hurry by with ladder and with
light,
O Leerie, see a little child and nod to him
to-night !

·MY·BED·IS· ·A·BOAT·

 BED is like a little boat;
Nurse helps me in when I em-
bark;
She girds me in my sailor's coat
And starts me in the dark.

At night, I go on board and say
Good-night to all my friends on shore;
I shut my eyes and sail away
And see and hear no more.

And sometimes things to bed I take,
As prudent sailors have to do:
Perhaps a slice of wedding-cake,
Perhaps a toy or two.

57

MY BED IS A BOAT

All night across the dark we steer:
　　But when the day returns at last,
Safe in my room, beside the pier,
　　I find my vessel fast.

THE moon has a face like the clock in the
hall;
She shines on thieves on the garden wall,
On streets and fields and harbour quays,
And birdies asleep in the forks of the trees.

The squalling cat and the squeaking mouse,
The howling dog by the door of the house,
The bat that lies in bed at noon,
All love to be out by the light of the moon.

The·moon·
has·a·
face·like·
the·
clock·in·
the·hall;

60

THE MOON

But all of the things that belong to the day
Cuddle to sleep to be out of her way;
And flowers and children close their eyes
Till up in the morning the sun shall arise.

THE SWING.

H OW do you like to go up in a
swing,
Up in the air so blue?
Oh, I do think it the pleasantest thing
Ever a child can do!

Up in the air and over the wall,
Till I can see so wide,
Rivers and trees and cattle and all
Over the countryside—

THE SWING

Till I look down on the garden green,
   Down on the roof so brown—
Up in the air I go flying again,
   Up in the air and down!

TIME TO RISE ·

A BIRDIE
with a yellow bill
Hopped upon the window
sill,
Cocked his shining eye and
said:
'Ain't you 'shamed, you
sleepy-head?'

LOOKING-GLASS RIVER

SMOOTH it slides upon its travel,
　　Here a wimple, there a gleam—
　　　　O the clean gravel!
　　　　O the smooth stream!

　Sailing blossoms, silver fishes,
　　Paven pools as clear as air—
　　　　How a child wishes
　　　　To live down there!

　We can see our coloured faces
　　Floating on the shaken pool
　　　　Down in cool places,
　　　　Dim and very cool;

LOOKING-GLASS RIVER

Till a wind or water wrinkle,
  Dipping marten, plumping trout,
    Spreads in a twinkle
    And blots all out.

See the rings pursue each other;
  All below grows black as night,
    Just as if mother
    Had blown out the light!

Patience, children, just a minute—
  See the spreading circles die;
    The stream and all in it
    Will clear by-and-by.

FAIRY~BREAD

COME up here, O dusty feet!
  Here is fairy bread to eat.
Here in my retiring room,
  Children you may dine
On the golden smell of broom
  And the shade of pine;
And when you have eaten well,
Fairy stories hear and tell.

67

FASTER than fairies, faster than
witches,
    Bridges and houses, hedges and
        ditches;
And charging along like troops in a battle,
All through the meadows the horses and cattle:
All of the sights of the hill and the plain
Fly as thick as driving rain;
And ever again, in the wink of an eye,
Painted stations whistle by.

Here is a child who clambers and scrambles,
All by himself and gathering brambles;
Here is a tramp who stands and gazes;
And there is the green for stringing the daisies!

68

FROM A RAILWAY CARRIAGE

Here is a cart run away in the road
Lumping along with man and load ;
And here is a mill and there is a river :
Each a glimpse and gone for ever !

LATE lies the wintry sun a-bed,
　　A frosty, fiery sleepy-head;
Blinks but an hour or two; and then,
A blood-red orange, sets again.

Before the stars have left the skies,
At morning in the dark I rise;
And shivering in my nakedness,
By the cold candle, bathe and dress.

WINTER-TIME

Close by the jolly fire I sit
To warm my frozen bones a bit;
Or, with a reindeer-sled, explore
The colder countries round the door.

When to go out, my nurse doth wrap
Me in my comforter and cap:
The cold wind burns my face, and blows
Its frosty pepper up my nose.

Black are my steps on silver sod;
Thick blows my frosty breath abroad;
And tree and house, and hill and lake,
Are frosted like a wedding-cake.

THE HAYLOFT

THROUGH all the pleasant meadow-side
  The grass grew shoulder-high,
   Till the shining scythes went far and
        wide
And cut it down to dry.

These green and sweetly smelling crops
  They led in waggons home;
And they piled them here in mountain tops
  For mountaineers to roam.

Here is Mount Clear, Mount Rusty-Nail,
  Mount Eagle and Mount High;—
The mice that in these mountains dwell,
  No happier are than I!

THE HAYLOFT

O what a joy to clamber there,
  O what a place for play,
With the sweet, the dim, the dusty air,
  The happy hills of hay.

FAREWELL·TO·THE FARM·

HE coach is at the door at last;
The eager children, mounting fast
And kissing hands, in chorus sing:
Good-bye, good-bye, to everything!

To house and garden, field and lawn,
The meadow-gates we swang upon,
To pump and stable, tree and swing,
Good-bye, good-bye, to everything!

And fare you well for evermore,
O ladder at the hayloft door,
O hayloft, where the cobwebs cling,
Good-bye, good-bye, to everything!

FAREWELL TO THE FARM

Crack goes the whip, and off we go ;
The trees and houses smaller grow ;
Last, round the woody turn we swing :
Good-bye, good-bye, to everything !

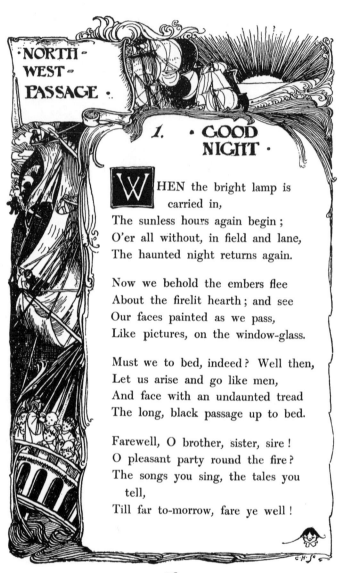

NORTH · WEST · PASSAGE

1. · GOOD NIGHT ·

WHEN the bright lamp is
carried in,
The sunless hours again begin;
O'er all without, in field and lane,
The haunted night returns again.

Now we behold the embers flee
About the firelit hearth; and see
Our faces painted as we pass,
Like pictures, on the window-glass.

Must we to bed, indeed? Well then,
Let us arise and go like men,
And face with an undaunted tread
The long, black passage up to bed.

Farewell, O brother, sister, sire!
O pleasant party round the fire?
The songs you sing, the tales you
tell,
Till far to-morrow, fare ye well!

76

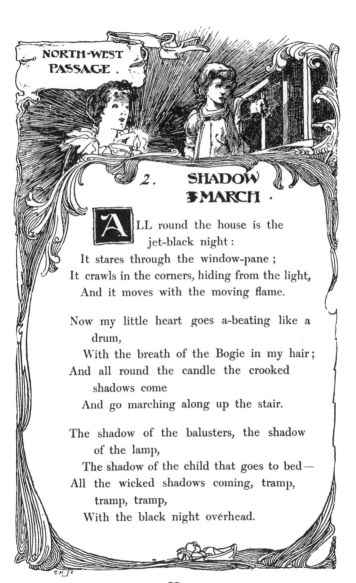

2. SHADOW MARCH .

ALL round the house is the
    jet-black night :
It stares through the window-pane ;
It crawls in the corners, hiding from the light,
    And it moves with the moving flame.

Now my little heart goes a-beating like a
    drum,
    With the breath of the Bogie in my hair ;
And all round the candle the crooked
    shadows come
    And go marching along up the stair.

The shadow of the balusters, the shadow
    of the lamp,
    The shadow of the child that goes to bed—
All the wicked shadows coming, tramp,
    tramp, tramp,
    With the black night overhead.

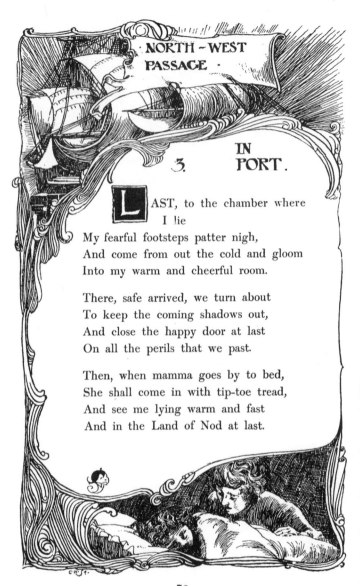

NORTH ~ WEST PASSAGE

3. IN PORT.

LAST, to the chamber where
    I lie
My fearful footsteps patter nigh,
And come from out the cold and gloom
Into my warm and cheerful room.

There, safe arrived, we turn about
To keep the coming shadows out,
And close the happy door at last
On all the perils that we past.

Then, when mamma goes by to bed,
She shall come in with tip-toe tread,
And see me lying warm and fast
And in the Land of Nod at last.

THE CHILD ALONE.

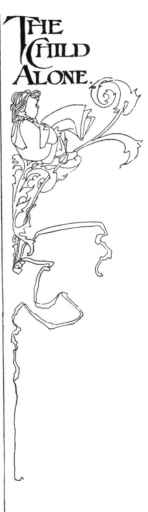

THE UNSEEN PLAYMATE

WHEN children are playing alone on the
green,
In comes the playmate that never was seen.
When children are happy and lonely and good,
The Friend of the Children comes out of the
wood.

Nobody heard him and nobody saw,
His is a picture you never could draw,
But he's sure to be present, abroad or at home,
When children are happy and playing alone.

He lies in the laurels, he runs on the grass,
He sings when you tinkle the musical glass;

THE UNSEEN PLAYMATE

Whene'er you are happy and cannot tell why
The Friend of the Children is sure to be by!

He loves to be little, he hates to be big,
'T is he that inhabits the caves that you dig;
'T is he when you play with your soldiers of tin
That sides with the Frenchmen and never can win.

'T is he, when at night you go off to your bed,
Bids you go to your sleep and not trouble your
    head;
For wherever they're lying, in cupboard or shelf,
'T is he will take care of your playthings himself!

MY SHIP
AND I

O IT'S I that am the captain of a tidy little
  ship,
Of a ship that goes a-sailing on the pond;
And my ship it keeps a-turning all around and all
    about;
But when I'm a little older, I shall find the secret
    out
  How to send my vessel sailing on beyond.

For I mean to grow as little as the dolly at the
    helm,
  And the dolly I intend to come alive;
And with him beside to help me, it's a-sailing I
    shall go,
It's a-sailing on the water, when the jolly breezes
    blow,
  And the vessel goes a divie-divie-dive.

83

O it's then you'll see me sailing through the
    rushes and the reeds,
  And you'll hear the water singing at the prow;
For beside the dolly sailor, I'm to voyage and
    explore,
To land upon the island where no dolly was
    before,
  And to fire the penny cannon in the bow.

MY KINGDOM.

DOWN by a shining water well
   I found a very little dell,
     No higher than my head.
The heather and the gorse about
In summer bloom were coming out,
     Some yellow and some red.

I called the little pool a sea ;
   The little hills were big to me ;
     For I am very small.
I made a boat, I made a town,
I searched the caverns up and down,
     And named them one and all.

And all about was mine, I said,
The little sparrows overhead,
     The little minnows too.
This was the world and I was king ;
For me the bees came by to sing,
     For me the swallows flew.

MY KINGDOM

I played, there were no deeper seas,
Nor any wider plains than these,
    Nor other kings than me.
At last I heard my mother call
Out from the house at evenfall,
    To call me home to tea.

And I must rise and leave my dell,
And leave my dimpled water well,
    And leave my heather blooms.
Alas! and as my home I neared,
How very big my nurse appeared,
    How great and cool the rooms!

PICTURE BOOKS
IN WINTER.

SUMMER fading, winter comes—
Frosty mornings, tingling thumbs,
Window robins, winter rooks,
And the picture story-books.

Water now is turned to stone
Nurse and I can walk upon;
Still we find the flowing brooks
In the picture story-books.

All the pretty things put by,
Wait upon the children's eye,
Sheep and shepherds, trees and crooks
In the picture story-books.

PICTURE BOOKS IN WINTER

We may see how all things are,
Seas and cities, near and far,
And the flying fairies' looks,
In the picture story-books.

How am I to sing your praise,
Happy chimney-corner days,
Sitting safe in nursery nooks,
Reading picture story-books?

MY TREASURES.

THESE nuts, that I keep in the back of the
    nest
Where all my lead soldiers are lying at rest,
Were gathered in autumn by nursie and me
In a wood with a well by the side of the sea.

This whistle was made (and how clearly it sounds !)
By the side of a field at the end of the grounds.
Of a branch of a plane, with a knife of my own—
It was nursie who made it, and nursie alone !

MY TREASURES

The stone, with the white and the yellow and grey,
We discovered I cannot tell *how* far away;
And I carried it back although weary and cold,
For though father denies it, I'm sure it is gold.

But of all of my treasures the last is the king,
For there's very few children possess such a thing;
And that is a chisel, both handle and blade,
Which a man who was really a carpenter made.

BLOCK CITY.

WHAT are you able to build with your blocks?
Castles and palaces, temples and docks.
Rain may keep raining, and others go roam,
But I can be happy and building at home.

Let the sofa be mountains, the carpet be sea,
There I'll establish a city for me:
A kirk and a mill and a palace beside,
And a harbour as well where my vessels may ride.

Great is the palace with pillar and wall,
A sort of a tower on the top of it all,
And steps coming down in an orderly way
To where my toy vessels lie safe in the bay.

This one is sailing and that one is moored:
Hark to the song of the sailors on board!
And see on the steps of my palace, the kings
Coming and going with presents and things!

91

BLOCK CITY

Now I have done with it, down let it go!
All in a moment the town is laid low.
Block upon block lying scattered and free,
What is there left of my town by the sea?

Yet as I saw it, I see it again,
The kirk and the palace, the ships and the men,
And as long as I live and where'er I may be,
I'll always remember my town by the sea.

THE LAND OF STORY-BOOKS

A T evening, when the lamp is lit,
  Around the fire my parents sit;
They sit at home and talk and sing,
And do not play at anything.

Now, with my little gun, I crawl
All in the dark along the wall,
And follow round the forest track
Away behind the sofa back.

There, in the night, where none can spy,
All in my hunter's camp I lie,
And play at books that I have read
Till it is time to go to bed.

These are the hills, these are the woods,
These are my starry solitudes;
And there the river by whose brink
The roaring lions come to drink.

THE LAND OF STORY-BOOKS

I see the others far away
As if in firelit camp they lay,
And I, like to an Indian scout,
Around their party prowled about.

So, when my nurse comes in for me,
Home I return across the sea,
And go to bed with backward looks
At my dear land of Story-books.

ARMIES IN THE FIRE.

THE lamps now glitter down the street;
  Faintly sound the falling feet;
And the blue even slowly falls
About the garden trees and walls.

Now in the falling of the gloom
The red fire paints the empty room:
And warmly on the roof it looks,
And flickers on the backs of books.

Armies march by tower and spire
Of cities blazing, in the fire;
Till as I gaze with staring eyes,
The armies fade, the lustre dies.

ARMIES IN THE FIRE

Then once again the glow returns;
Again the phantom city burns;
And down the red-hot valley, lo!
The phantom armies marching go!

Blinking embers, tell me true,
Where are those armies marching to,
And what the burning city is
That crumbles in your furnaces!

·THE·LITTLE·LAND·

WHEN at home alone I sit
    And am very tired of it,
I have just to shut my eyes
To go sailing through the skies—
To go sailing far away
To the pleasant Land of Play;
To the fairy land afar
Where the little people are;
Where the clover-tops are trees,
And the rain-pools are the seas,
And the leaves like little ships
Sail about on tiny trips;
And above the daisy tree
    Through the grasses,
High o'erhead the Bumble Bee
    Hums and passes.

THE LITTLE LAND

In that forest to and fro
I can wander, I can go;
See the spider and the fly,
And the ants go marching by
Carrying parcels with their feet
Down the green and grassy street.
I can in the sorrel sit
Where the ladybird alit.
I can climb the jointed grass;
    And on high
See the greater swallows pass
    In the sky,
And the round sun rolling by
Heeding no such things as I.

Through that forest I can pass
Till, as in a looking glass,
Humming fly and daisy tree
And my tiny self I see,

THE LITTLE LAND

Painted very clear and neat
On the rain-pool at my feet.
Should a leaflet come to land
Drifting near to where I stand,
Straight I'll board that tiny boat
Round the rain-pool sea to float.

Little thoughtful creatures sit
On the grassy coasts of it;
Little things with lovely eyes
See me sailing with surprise.
Some are clad in armour green—
(These have sure to battle been!)—
Some are pied with ev'ry hue,
Black and crimson, gold and blue;
Some have wings and swift are gone;—
But they all look kindly on.

When my eyes I once again
Open, and see all things plain:
High bare walls, great bare floor;

THE LITTLE LAND

Great big knobs on drawer and door;
Great big people perched on chairs,
Stitching tucks and mending tears,
Each a hill that I could climb,
And talking nonsense all the time—
    O dear me,
    That I could be
A sailor on the rain-pool sea,
A climber in the clover-tree,
And just come back, a sleepy head,
Late at night to go to bed.

GARDEN
DAYS.

NIGHT
AND
DAY.

WHEN the golden day
　　is done,
Through the closing portal,
Child and garden, flower and sun,
　Vanish all things mortal.

103

NIGHT AND DAY

As the blinding shadows fall,
  As the rays diminish,
Under the evening's cloak, they all
  Roll away and vanish.

Garden darkened, daisy shut,
  Child in bed, they slumber—
Glow-worm in the highway rut,
  Mice among the lumber.

In the darkness houses shine,
  Parents move with candles ;
Till on all, the night divine
  Turns the bedroom handles.

NIGHT AND DAY

Till at last the day begins
  In the east a-breaking,
In the hedges and the whins
  Sleeping birds a-waking.

In the darkness shapes of things,
  Houses, trees, and hedges
Clearer grow ; and sparrow's wings
  Beat on window ledges.

These shall wake the yawning maid ;
  She the door shall open—
Finding dew on garden glade
  And the morning broken.

There my garden grows again
  Green and rosy painted,
As at eve behind the pane
  From my eyes it fainted.

Just as it was shut away,
  Toy-like, in the even,
Here I see it glow with day
  Under glowing heaven.

NIGHT AND DAY

Every path and every plot,
  Every bush of roses,
Every blue forget-me-not
  Where the dew reposes,

"Up!" they cry, "the day is come
  On the smiling valleys:
We have beat the morning drum;
  Playmate, join your allies!"

NEST EGGS.

BIRDS all the sunny day
   Flutter and quarrel
Here in the arbour-like
   Tent of the laurel.

Here in the fork
   The brown nest is seated;
Four little blue eggs
   The mother keeps heated.

107

NEST EGGS

While we stand watching her,
   Staring like gabies,
Safe in each egg are the
   Bird's little babies.

Soon the frail eggs they shall
   Chip, and upspringing
Make all the April woods
   Merry with singing.

Younger than we are,
   O children, and frailer,
Soon in blue air they'll be,
   Singer and sailor.

We, so much older,
   Taller and stronger,
We shall look down on the
   Birdies no longer.

They shall go flying
   With musical speeches
High overhead in the
   Tops of the beeches.

NEST EGGS

In spite of our wisdom
And sensible talking,
We on our feet must go
Plodding and walking.

THE·FLOWERS

ALL the names I know from nurse:
  Gardener's garters, Shepherd's purse;
Bachelor's buttons, Lady's smock,
And the Lady Hollyhock.

Fairy places, fairy things,
Fairy woods where the wild bee wings,
Tiny trees for tiny dames—
These must all be fairy names!

THE FLOWERS

Tiny woods below whose boughs
Shady fairies weave a house ;
Tiny tree tops, rose or thyme,
Where the braver fairies climb !

Fair are grown-up people's trees,
But the fairest woods are these ;
Where, if I were not so tall,
I should live for good and all.

SUMMER SUN.

G REAT is the sun, and wide he goes
  Through empty heaven without repose;
And in the blue and glowing days
More thick than rain he showers his rays.

SUMMER SUN

Though closer still the blinds we pull
To keep the shady parlour cool,
Yet he will find a chink or two
To slip his golden fingers through.

The dusty attic spider-clad
He, through the keyhole, maketh glad;
And through the broken edge of tiles,
Into the laddered hayloft smiles.

Meantime his golden face around
He bares to all the garden ground,
And sheds a warm and glittering look
Among the ivy's inmost nook.

Above the hills, along the blue,
Round the bright air with footing true,
To please the child, to paint the rose,
The gardener of the World, he goes.

THE DUMB SOLDIER

WHEN the grass was closely mown,
  Walking on the lawn alone,
In the turf a hole I found
And hid a soldier underground.

THE DUMB SOLDIER

Spring and daisies came apace;
Grasses hide my hiding place;
Grasses run like a green sea
O'er the lawn up to my knee.

Under grass alone he lies,
Looking up with leaden eyes,
Scarlet coat and pointed gun,
To the stars and to the sun.

When the grass is ripe like grain,
When the scythe is stoned again,
When the lawn is shaven clear,
Then my hole shall reappear.

I shall find him, never fear,
I shall find my grenadier;
But for all that's gone and come,
I shall find my soldier dumb.

He has lived, a little thing,
In the grassy woods of spring;
Done, if he could tell me true,
Just as I should like to do.

THE DUMB SOLDIER

He has seen the starry hours
And the springing of the flowers;
And the fairy things that pass
In the forests of the grass.

In the silence he has heard
Talking bee and ladybird,
And the butterfly has flown
O'er him as he lay alone.

Not a word will he disclose,
Not a word of all he knows.
I must lay him on the shelf,
And make up the tale myself.

AUTUMN FIRES

I N the other gardens
    And all up the vale,
From the autumn bonfires
    See the smoke trail !

Pleasant summer over
  And all the summer flowers,
The red fire blazes,
  The grey smoke towers.

Sing a song of seasons!
  Something bright in all!
Flowers in the summer,
  Fires in the fall!

THE GARDENER

THE gardener does not love to talk,
  He makes me keep the gravel walk;
And when he puts his tools away,
He locks the door and takes the key.

Away behind the currant row
Where no one else but cook may go,
Far in the plots, I see him dig,
Old and serious, brown and big.

He digs the flowers, green, red and blue,
Nor wishes to be spoken to.
He digs the flowers and cuts the hay,
And never seems to want to play.

THE GARDENER

Silly gardener ! summer goes,
And winter comes with pinching toes,
When in the garden bare and brown
You must lay your barrow down.

Well now, and while the summer stays,
To profit by these garden days,
O how much wiser you would be
To play at Indian wars with me !

HISTORICAL ASSOCIATIONS.

DEAR Uncle Jim, this garden ground
    That now you smoke your pipe around,
Has seen immortal actions done
And valiant battles lost and won.

Here we had best on tip-toe tread,
While I for safety march ahead,
For this is that enchanted ground
Where all who loiter slumber sound.

Here is the sea, here is the sand,
Here is simple Shepherd's Land,
Here are the fairy hollyhocks,
And there are Ali Baba's rocks.

But yonder, see ! apart and high,
Frozen Siberia lies ; where I,
With Robert Bruce and William Tell,
Was bound by an enchanter's spell.

HISTORICAL ASSOCIATIONS

There, then, awhile in chains we lay,
In wintry dungeons, far from day ;
But ris'n at length, with might and main,
Our iron fetters burst in twain.

Then all the horns were blown in town ;
And to the ramparts clanging down,
All the giants leaped to horse
And charged behind us through the gorse.

On we rode, the others and I,
Over the mountains blue, and by
The Silver River, the sounding sea,
And the robber woods of Tartary.

A thousand miles we galloped fast,
And down the witches' lane we passed,
And rode amain with brandished sword,
Up to the middle, through the ford.

Last we drew rein—a weary three—
Upon the lawn, in time for tea,
And from our steeds alighted down
Before the gates of Babylon.

ENVOYS.

TO WILLIE AND HENRIETTA

I F two may read aright
    These rhymes of old delight
  And house and garden play,
You two, my cousins, and you only, may.

  You in a garden green
  With me were king and queen,
  Were hunter, soldier, tar,
And all the thousand things that children are.

  Now in the elders' seat
  We rest with quiet feet,
  And from the window-bay
We watch the children, our successors, play.

"Time was," the golden head
Irrevocably said ;
But time which none can bind,
While flowing fast away, leaves love behind.

TO MY ~
MOTHER.

YOU too, my mother, read my rhymes
For love of unforgotten times,
And you may chance to hear once more
The little feet along the floor.

·TO AUNTIE·

CHIEF of our aunts — not only I,
    But all your dozen of nurslings cry —
What did the other children do?
And what were childhood, wanting you?

TO MINNIE

THE red room with the giant bed
    Where none but elders laid their head;
The little room where you and I
Did for awhile together lie
And, simple suitor, I your hand
In decent marriage did demand;
The great day nursery, best of all,
With pictures pasted on the wall
And leaves upon the blind—
A pleasant room wherein to wake
And hear the leafy garden shake
And rustle in the wind—

And pleasant there to lie in bed
And see the pictures overhead—
The wars about Sebastopol,
The grinning guns along the wall,
The daring escalade,
The plunging ships, the bleating sheep,
The happy children ankle-deep
And laughing as they wade:
All these are vanished clean away,
And the old manse is changed to-day;
It wears an altered face
And shields a stranger race.
The river, on from mill to mill,
Flows past our childhood's garden still;
But ah! we children never more
Shall watch it from the water-door!
Below the yew—it still is there—
Our phantom voices haunt the air
As we were still at play,
And I can hear them call and say:
'How far is it to Babylon?'

TO MINNIE

Ah, far enough, my dear,
Far, far enough from here—
Yet you have farther gone!
'*Can I get there by candlelight ?*'
So goes the old refrain.
I do not know—perchance you might—
But only, children, hear it right,
Ah, never to return again!
The eternal dawn, beyond a doubt,
Shall break on hill and plain,
And put all stars and candles out,
Ere we be young again.
To you in distant India, these
I send across the seas,
Nor count it far across.
For which of us forgets
The Indian cabinets,
The bones of antelope, the wings of albatross,
The pied and painted birds and beans,
The junks and bangles, beads and screens,
The gods and sacred bells,
And the loud-humming, twisted shells?
The level of the parlour floor
Was honest, homely, Scottish shore ;
But when we climbed upon a chair,
Behold the gorgeous East was there !
Be this a fable ; and behold
Me in the parlour as of old,
And Minnie just above me set
In the quaint Indian cabinet !

TO MINNIE

Smiling and kind, you grace a shelf
Too high for me to reach myself.
Reach down a hand, my dear, and take
These rhymes for old acquaintance' sake.

TO MY NAME-CHILD

1

SOME day soon this rhyming volume, if you
learn with proper speed,
Little Louis Sanchez, will be given you to read.
Then shall you discover that your name was
printed down
By the English printers, long before, in London
town.

In the great and busy city where the East and
West are met,
All the little letters did the English printer set;

TO MY NAME-CHILD

While you thought of nothing, and were still too
    young to play,
Foreign people thought of you in places far away.

Ay, and while you slept, a baby, over all the
    English lands
Other little children took the volume in their
    hands ;
Other children questioned, in their homes across
    the seas :
Who was little Louis, won't you tell us, mother,
    please ?

2

Now that you have spelt your lesson, lay it down
    and go and play,
Seeking shells and seaweed on the sands of
    Monterey,

TO MY NAME-CHILD

Watching all the mighty whalebones, lying buried
    by the breeze,
Tiny sandy-pipers, and the huge Pacific seas.

And remember in your playing, as the sea-fog rolls
    to you,
Long ere you could read it, how I told you what
    to do ;
And that while you thought of no one, nearly half
    the world away
Some one thought of Louis on the beach of
    Monterey !

TO
ANY
READER.

A S from the house your mother sees
You playing round the garden trees,
So you may see, if you will look
Through the windows of this book,
Another child, far, far away,
And in another garden, play.
But do not think you can at all,
By knocking on the window, call
That child to hear you. He intent
Is all on his play-business bent.
He does not hear; he will not look,
Nor yet be lured out of this book.

TO ANY READER

For, long ago, the truth to say,
He has grown up and gone away,
And it is but a child of air
That lingers in the garden there.

THE END

Robert Louis Stevenson:

AN ELEGY.

And other Poems, mainly Personal.

By Richard Le Gallienne.

**With Etched Frontispiece, containing Vignette
Portrait of Stevenson by D. Y. Cameron.**

Crown 8vo, 4s. 6d. net.

Also 75 Large-paper Copies, Demy 8vo, 12s. 6d. net.

"*Few, indeed, could be more fit to sing the dirge of that ' Virgil
of prose' than the poet whose* curiosa felicitas *is so :lose akin to
Stevenson's own charm.*"—DAILY CHRONICLE.

"*The graceful and sonorous Elegy to Robert Louis Stevenson, with
which this volume opens, appears to us to strike a truer and a deeper
note than we have hitherto been able to discern in Mr. Le Gallienne's
verse.*"—TIMES.

"*The opening Elegy on R. L. Stevenson includes some tender and
touching passages, and has throughout the merits of sincerity and
clearness.*"—GLOBE.

"*The Ode is fresh, apposite to Stevenson's genius, and finely
phrased.*"—MANCHESTER GUARDIAN.

"*The Elegy on Stevenson is a not unworthy companion to the three
or four great elegies that are counted best in our literature.*"—STAR.

"*The Elegy is deserving of the highest praise. It is just without
being fulsome, and it is sincere.*"—ST. JAMES'S BUDGET.

"*The Elegy on Stevenson, for sensitive harmony with its subject,
stands with honour among the not very numerous fine poems of its
kind.*"—BOOKMAN.

"*It is what an elegy should be: passionate, simple, and sincere.*'
IRISH DAILY INDEPENDENT.

"*The personal allusions to Stevenson, the picturesque touches that
bring before us his Samoan isle of refuge and final resting-place, are
delightfully wrought in.*"—YORKSHIRE HERALD.

Printed and bound in Great Britain by
The Bath Press, Bath

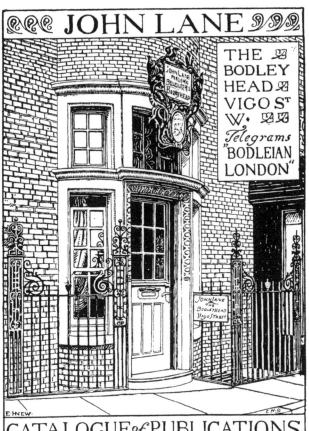

JOHN LANE

JOHN LANE
PUBLISHER
BELLES LETTRES
BODLEY HEAD

THE
BODLEY
HEAD
VIGO St
W.
Telegrams
"BODLEIAN
LONDON"

JOHN LANE
THE
BODLEY HEAD
VIGO STREET

E. H. NEW.

CATALOGUE *of* PUBLICATIONS
in BELLES LETTRES *all at net prices*

List of Books

IN

BELLES LETTRES

(Including some Transfers)

Published by John Lane

The Bodley Head

Vigo Street, London, W.

N.B.—The Authors and Publisher reserve the right of reprinting any book in this list if a new edition is called for, except in cases where a stipulation has been made to the contrary, and of printing a separate edition of any of the books for America irrespective of the numbers to which the English editions are limited. The numbers mentioned do not include copies sent to the public libraries, nor those sent for review.

Most of the books are published simultaneously in England and America, and in many instances the names of the American publishers are appended.

ADAMS (FRANCIS).

ESSAYS IN MODERNITY. Cr. 8vo. 5s. net. [*Shortly.*
Chicago: Stone & Kimball.

A CHILD OF THE AGE. (*See* KEYNOTES SERIES.)

ALLEN (GRANT).

THE LOWER SLOPES : A Volume of Verse. With title-page and cover design by J. ILLINGWORTH KAY. 600 copies, cr. 8vo. 5s. net.
Chicago: Stone & Kimball.

THE WOMAN WHO DID. (*See* KEYNOTES SERIES.)

THE BRITISH BARBARIANS. (*See* KEYNOTES SERIES.)

BAILEY (JOHN C.).

AN ANTHOLOGY OF ENGLISH ELEGIES.   [*In preparation.*

BEARDSLEY (AUBREY).

THE STORY OF VENUS AND TANNHÄUSER, in which is set
forth an exact account of the Manner of State held by
Madam Venus, Goddess and Meretrix, under the famous
Hörselberg, and containing the adventures of Tannhäuser
in that place, his repentance, his journeying to Rome, and
return to the loving mountain. By AUBREY BEARDSLEY.
With 20 full-page illustrations, numerous ornaments, and
a cover from the same hand. Sq. 16mo. 10s. 6d. *net.*
                                                    [*In preparation.*

BEDDOES (T. L.).

See GOSSE (EDMUND).

BEECHING (Rev. H. C.).

IN A GARDEN : Poems. With title-page and cover design by
ROGER FRY. Cr. 8vo. 5s. *net.*
New York: Macmillan & Co.

BENSON (ARTHUR CHRISTOPHER).

LYRICS. Fcap. 8vo, buckram. 5s. *net.*
New York: Macmillan & Co.

BRIDGES (ROBERT).

SUPPRESSED CHAPTERS, AND OTHER BOOKISHNESS. Cr. 8vo,
3s. 6d. *net.*
New York : Charles Scribner's Sons.

BROTHERTON (MARY).

ROSEMARY FOR REMEMBRANCE. With title-page and cover
design by WALTER WEST. Fcap. 8vo. 3s. 6d. *net.*

BUCHAN (JOHN).

MUSA PISCATRIX.   [*In preparation.*

CAMPBELL (GERALD).

THE JONESES AND THE ASTERISKS. (*See* MAYFAIR SET.)

CASE (ROBERT).

AN ANTHOLOGY OF ENGLISH EPITHALAMIES.
                                                    [*In preparation.*

CASTLE (Mrs. EGERTON).

MY LITTLE LADY ANNE. (*See* PIERROT'S LIBRARY.)

CASTLE (EGERTON).
> *See* STEVENSON (ROBERT LOUIS).

CRAIG (R. MANIFOLD).
> THE SACRIFICE OF FOOLS : A Novel.   Cr. 8vo.   4s. 6d. net.
> *[In preparation.*

CRANE (WALTER).
> TOY BOOKS.   Re-issue.   Each with new cover-design and end
>> papers.   9d. net.
>> The three bound in one volume with a decorative cloth cover,
>> end papers, and a newly-written and designed title-page
>> and preface.   3s. 6d. net.   i. This Little Pig.   ii. The Fairy
>> Ship.   iii. King Luckieboy's Party.
> *Chicago: Stone & Kimball.*

CROSSE (VICTORIA).
> THE WOMAN WHO DIDN'T.   (*See* KEYNOTES SERIES.)

DALMON (C. W.).
> SONG FAVOURS.   With a title-page designed by J. P. DONNE.
>> Sq. 16mo.   3s. 6d. net.
> *Chicago: Way & Williams.*

D'ARCY (ELLA).
> MONOCHROMES.   (*See* KEYNOTES SERIES.)

DAVIDSON (JOHN).
> PLAYS :   An Unhistorical Pastoral ;   A Romantic Farce ;
>> Bruce, a Chronicle Play ;   Smith, a Tragic Farce ;   Scara-
>> mouch in Naxos, a Pantomime.   With a frontispiece and
>> cover design by AUBREY BEARDSLEY.   Printed at the
>> Ballantyne Press.   500 copies, sm. 4to.   7s. 6d. net.
> *Chicago: Stone & Kimball.*

> FLEET STREET ECLOGUES.   Fcap. 8vo, buckram   4s. 6d. *net.*
>> *[Third Edition.*

> FLEET STREET ECLOGUES.   Second Series.   Fcap. 8vo, buck-
>> ram.   4s. 6d. net.

> A RANDOM ITINERARY AND A BALLAD.   With a frontispiece
>> and title-page by LAURENCE HOUSMAN.   600 copies.
>> Fcap. 8vo, Irish Linen.   5s. *net.*
> *Boston : Copeland & Day.*

> BALLADS AND SONGS.   With title-page designed by WALTER
>> WEST.   Fourth Edition.   Fcap. 8vo, buckram.   5s. *net*
> *Boston : Copeland & Day.*

DAWE (W. CARLTON).
> YELLOW AND WHITE.   (*See* KEYNOTES SERIES.)